IT'S OUR HERITAGE FROM THE DREAMTIME 2

IN SEARCH OF TANGAROA

SEMISI PONE
BSc, MSc (Hons)

Copyright © Rainbow Enterprises Books

Publisher: Rainbow Enterprises Books

ISBN: 978-1-98-851108-5

No part of this book shall be reproduced, in any way, without prior written permission from the writer and copyright holder.

Rainbow Enterprises Books is a division of Rainbow Enterprises and Investments 7 Ltd

Please Note: Much of the information in this book were derived from Wikipedia, the free online encyclopedia and is marked with a *.

CONTENTS

Introduction

Chapter 1. The Thor Heyerdahl Theory

Chapter 2. The Asian Connection

Chapter 3. The South American Civilizations

Chapter 4. Raiatea and Hawaiki

Chapter 5. Tangaloa 'Eitumatupu'a the Tongan legend

Chapter 6. Another Meaning of the Legend

INTRODUCTION

Since I was a child, the story of Tangaroa has always fascinated me. In Tongan oral history Tangaroa came down from the sky and married a Tongan woman giving rise to the first Tu'i Tonga. The beginning of the Tu'i Tonga Dynasty around the year 950 which lasted until 1865.

Many other lineage of Kings arose from the Tu'i Tonga, being appointed to share the administration job as the population gets bigger.

Tangaroa is also famous around the Pacific Polynesian Islands as a God with many talents. Each island has a special place for the Polynesian God Tangaroa.

This book will examine my theory that it is possible Tangaroa was a voyager explorer who came from a higher civilization. His superior knowledge in many things endeared him to the islanders as a God.

This book is a discussion of the evidence and the possibility that Tangaroa and his fellow travellers 'Aho'eitu and Tupu'a who are collectively known as Tangaroa 'Eitumatupu'a in Tonga (Tangaroa, 'Aho'eitu and Tupu'a) came from either Asia or South America, but most probably South America, and travelled the Pacific islands before settling in Samoa, Tonga and New Zealand. They were accompanied by a white woman Hina or Sina. Or perhaps like Lo'au, they left and never returned.

In other islands Tangaroa's companions are referred to by various names but the most significant ones to this investigation is the Maori legend that Papa and Rangi were Tangaroa's brothers, who used to accompany him around New Zealand and probably the Pacific. It is possible they are 'Eitu ('Aho'eitu) and Tupu'a in Tongan folklore. In the Cook islands they are referred to as Rongo and Tane. Cook island Mythology suggest that Tangaroa and twin Rongo were the children of Papa and Avatea, the primal parents. Avatea refers to 'white vagina', it is possible that Tangaroa's mother was a white woman. This Tangaroa could be a nephew of the Maori Tangaroa, whose brother is Papa.

In Polynesia especially Tonga and Samoa, the white people are called 'papalangi' (Papa and Rangi) and usually shortened to 'palangi'. There is direct connection here to the White Gods of South America that disappeared into the Pacific (Thor Heyerdahl's accounts)….and gave rise to the name 'papalangi' in Polynesia.

As you read through the Thor Heyerdahl account, it will become apparent that Tangaroa, Papa ('Eitu) and Rangi (Tupu'a) and many other Gods of the Polynesians (Tane, Rono, Whiru and even Maui) may have originated in South America. The White Gods that once lived there and mysteriously disappeared into the Pacific Ocean.

CHAPTER 1. The Thor Heyerdahl Theory

Thor Heyerdahl was a Norwegian scholar, writer and academic with a background in zoology, botany and geography. In 1947, he build a raft made of balsa wood and sailed from Peru to the Pacific Islands to prove that the Polynesians came from South America. His raft the 'Kon-tiki', named after the Inca Sun God, sailed from Peru on April 28, 1947 and arrived at Raroia, Tuamotu Islands in French Polynesia on August 7, 1947, before they hit the reef at Raroia they had sighted 2 other islands days before. They had sailed 6,900 kilometres over 101 days. It proved to the world that it was possible for some of the ancient Polynesians to have come from South America.

There were also many other expeditions, after the Kon-tiki, from South America to Polynesia which were all successful and proving beyond a reasonable doubt that some of the Polynesian's ancestors came from South America.

Thor Heyerdahl also argued that the people of Easter Island were from South America. DNA evidence from research presented in 2011 and 2014 suggested that Thor was right.

In 2014, work by a team from the Natural History Museum of Denmark analyzed genomes of 27 native people from Rapa Nui (Easter Island) and found them to be 76% Polynesian, 8% Native American and 16% European*. It was obvious that European contact left its mark since first contact with Europeans in 1722. The South American component was much older dating back to between 1200 to 1400 which was about the time the island was first colonized. There is also mention of ancient skulls found in Brazil which has Polynesian DNA*.

Heyerdahl had postulated that the island was inhabited by people from South America and a later wave of migration caused conflict which wiped out the islands once prosperous economy.

Thor Heyerdahl's Theory* Quote

Heyerdahl claimed that in Incan legend there was a sun-god named Kon Tiki. Kon-Tiki was also the name of the high priest and sun-king of these legendary "white men" who left enormous ruins on the shores of Lake Titicaca. The legend continues with the mysterious bearded white men being attacked by a chief named Cari, who came from the Coquimbo Valley. They had a battle on an island in Lake Titicaca and the fair race was massacred. However, Kon-Tiki and his closest companions managed to escape and later arrived on the Pacific coast. The legend ends with Kon-Tiki and his companions disappearing westward out to sea.

When the Spaniards came to Peru, Heyerdahl asserted, the Incas told them that the colossal monuments that stood deserted about the landscape were erected by a race of white gods who had lived there before the Incas themselves became rulers. The Incas described these "white gods" as wise, peaceful instructors who had originally come from the north in the "morning of time" and taught the Incas' primitive forebears architecture as well as manners and customs. They were unlike other Native Americans in that they had "white skins and long beards" and were taller than the Incas. The Incas said that the "white gods" had then left as suddenly as they had come and fled westward across the Pacific. After they had left, the Incas themselves took over power in the country. Unquote.

Most historians believe that Polynesia was settled from the waves of migrants from Asia and it is possible that these

'Polynesians' were the second wave of migrants to arrive on the Easter Island.

What Thor's Kon-Tiki expedition and his theory did was to support the idea that South America was also a source of migrants to the Pacific Islands.

The existence of the sweet potato and cassava in Polynesia also prove that there were migrants from South America in Polynesia. Sweet potato or kumara and cassava are native to South America*.

Excavations on the shores of South America also found evidence the Polynesians had camped on the beach there many hundreds of years ago*.

Thor Heyerdahl also proposed that his research had found there were a white race of people who were intelligent, skilled and taller than the Incas with long beard. This race of white people left the South American mainland, probably due to conflict with the invading Incas. Heyerdahl credited this race of 'white gods' with building of the huge headstones on Easter Island and the pyramids in the islands of the Pacific including Samoa and the Marquezas Islands. The white race left the South American continent around AD 400-500.

Thor Heyerdahl also did carbon dating of charcoals in an ancient camp fire at Easter Island which dated it to 400 AD, about the time the 'white Gods' left the South America mainland.

The legend of Tangaroa does suggest that he was a 'foreigner' with a white woman, Sina, who travelled around the Pacific on a paepae or large canoe made of balsa wood. He was the instigator or main force behind the establishment of the Tu'i Tonga Dynasty in Tonga, according to Tongan legend. There are also large stone monuments and pyramids in Tonga. One of the ancient king's burial pyramid is actually called the 'Paepae 'o Tele'a' or Paepae of Tele'a, which is shaped like a balsa raft with a wide base and 2 smaller rectangles on top! Is it possible that the white gods from South America also taught the Polynesians architecture and culture like they did the Incas?

Heyerdahl also pointed out that the Europeans arriving on Easter Island in 1722 were surprised that some of the people there had fair skin!*

The arrival of Tangaroa in Tonga was possibly earlier than the year 950. He had a relationship with 2 women and left 6 children there and 'returned to the sky' which meant he sailed away after.

The youngest of his children became the King or Tu'i Tonga, according to legend. Tangaroa was regarded as a God by the local Tongans. Tangaroa was also regarded as a God, by other Pacific Island people, probably because of his skill and intelligent knowledge.

CHAPTER 2. The Asian Connection

For years, it was generally accepted that Polynesians originated in modern-day Taiwan and began moving south and east about 4,000 years ago. This migration account is based on the research of linguists, the findings of archaeologists and some genetic analysis*.

There are many more theories and much more DNA evidence to support migration from Asia into the Pacific Islands.

Language, culture and many food plants used in the Polynesian Islands originate from Asia including coconuts, mango, banana, taro, plantain and yams the most important foods in pre-European times.

A study by T. Melton *et al* (1995) of Polynesian genetic affinities to populations of Asia used mitochondrial DNA (mDNA) markers. A total of 1037 individuals from 12 populations were screened for a special region in their genes.

Here's their simplified findings.

Quote
'Sequence-specific oligonucleotide probes that identify specific mDNA control region nucleotide substitutions were used to describe variation in individuals. The gene marker was not observed in northern Indians, Bangladeshis, or Pakistanis but was seen at low to moderate frequencies in the nine other Southeast Asian populations. Three substitutions in the control region have previously been observed at high frequency in Polynesian mDNAs; this "Polynesian motif" was observed in 20% of east Indonesians. mDNA types related to the Polynesian motif are highest in frequency in the corridor from Taiwan south through the Philippines and east Indonesia, and the highest diversity for these types is in Taiwan. These results are consistent with linguistic evidence of a Taiwanese origin for the proto-Polynesian expansion, which spread throughout Oceania by way of Indonesia'. Unquote

The result suggest that the mDNA was not found in Indians, Bangladeshis or Pakistanis. They were only found in Taiwanese, Phillipinos and East

Indonesians suggesting a Polynesian migration route through those countries.

DNA evidence from other studies also support the migration from Asia theory. They show that mitochondrial DNA (mDNA) found in many Polynesian population originated in Asia. They were present in 100% of Samoans, Maori and Niueans in the 150 sample study. Ninety three percent of the Polynesians in the study had the Asian mDNA suggesting some of their ancestors were Asian in origin*.

However, only 14% of coastal New Guineans had the mDNA and none of the Highlander New Guineans and Australian Aborigines studied had them suggesting there were contacts and migration along the coast of New Guinea. The Fijians showed 82% frequency which confirm their affinity to Polynesia. The evidence support the theory there were migrations from Asia into the Pacific, through these countries.

A study by M Kayser *et al* (2000) also show all Polynesian Y chromosomes can be traced back to Melanesia, although some of these Y-chromosome types originated in Asia. Together with other genetic and cultural evidence, they propose a new model of Polynesian origins that they call the 'slow-boat' model: Polynesian ancestors did originate from Asia/Taiwan but did not move rapidly through Melanesia; rather, they interacted with and mixed extensively with Melanesians, leaving behind their genes and incorporating many Melanesian genes before colonizing the Pacific*.

CHAPTER 3. The South American Civilizations

The Inca was probably the biggest empire in the world during pre-Columbian times, that is before the arrival of Christopher Columbus in North America on August 3, 1492.

The Inca Empire began around 1300-1400 in what is now modern Peru. It was conquered by the Spanish in the 1500s.

In Central America and Mexico the Maya and Aztecs have much, much older civilizations dating back 3,000 years so it is possible that the Inca of Peru also had a similar ancient existence. The Mayan and Aztec civilizations, like the Inca, were also conquered by the Spanish.

Is it possible that these ancient civilizations had interaction with the Pacific peoples?

It may be possible that travellers during ancient times may have come from these ancient civilizations into the Pacific.

CHAPTER 4. Raiatea and Hawaiki

Raiatea means 'bright sky' in Tahitian. In the Tongan language it is known as La'atea or Lai'atea so there is a connection of the two languages like most Polynesian languages.

Raiatea is the second largest island, after Tahiti, in French Polynesia.

Both Raiatea and Tahiti may have been the landing place and origin of the migrations from South America. Tahiti is referred to in the legends as Hawaiki* the origin of the Polynesian people. It is possible that this refers to the people who originated from South America, probably the children and grand-children of the White Gods of South America.

Kupe the first Maori to arrive in New Zealand had come from Hawaiki* as well as the second wave of Maori migration to New Zealand led by Toi*.

One of the early Maori to land in New Zealand was Nukutawhiti (Nuku Tahiti) which is a common name in Polynesia. There is also a legend of Nuku, who is a modern Lord and estate holder, in the Kingdom of Tonga.

The Legend of the 'Ulutolu (Three Heads)

Tongan historical accounts attribute the trick by Ngata, Nuku and Niukapu by tieing a mat around themselves and scaring the people of Hihifo, as the reason for Ngata's installation as Tu'i Kanokupolu, or King of Kanokupolu. That is, they appear as a man with three heads. Only people with a very low IQ would believe that. It is unlikely to be the reason, as Tongans of that time were regarded as skilled in making handicrafts, weapons, canoes and they would not be tricked easily. The more likely explanation is that the three heads signify some incredible power which has to be obeyed. Was it the symbol of Tangaloa 'Eitumatupu'a? The three persons? It is very common through Pacific history. Tangaroa was always accompanied by his two brothers or two of the Gods. The three lines of Kings in Tonga. That is the Tu'i Tonga, Tu'i Ha'a Takalaua, Tu'i Kanokupolu is an example.

As demonstrated by Thor Heyerdahl. The White Gods *paepae* may have come from Peru and landed in French Polynesia around 400-500 AD. They may have intermarried with the locals giving rise to a new race of people. Raiatea and Hawaiki were the bigger islands and logically the centre of commerce and activities for the White Gods and their offspring. From Raiatea and Hawaiki they spread to the Cook Islands, Samoa, Fiji, Tonga and New Zealand in the 900s. About the same time the Chinese build their 'dhows' and started trading down the coast and perhaps all the way to Taiwan, Indonesia, Phillipines, New Guinea, Melanesia and Polynesia.

The Maya, Aztec and Inca civilizations were perfectly capable of constructing some sea worthy craft for such voyages. Did they make the voyages too?

Evidence of appearance

Captain James Cook on his visits to the Tonga Islands in 1773, 1774 and 1777 kept referring to the Tongans as the 'Indians' which is probably their appearance comparable to other ethnic groups he has met. No doubt Captain James Cook thought the Tongans looked similar to the Indians in South America rather than the Melanesians and other Polynesians, who look more like the Malay or natives of Taiwan.

There is mention that the population of Easter Island in 1722 were a mixed race of white people, Indians and Polynesians. However, when Captain cook arrived on Easter Island, a few years later, the white race have disappeared*.

Captain James Cook also referred to the chiefs in Tonga as 'ariki' which is a word for chief in Raiatea and Hawaiki, and most of Eastern Polynesia. In Samoan, the word is 'ali'i, meaning a male person of high birth or chief. This could be the origin of 'eiki or chief in Tonga.

———————

Captain James Cooks account from The Journal of the Polynesian Society

On May 21 Cook walked through the island, and with his usual care noted down that the plantations were larger and more numerous than at Nomuka, most of them being enclosed so that the fences formed public roads. Near the sea there were no plantations, doubtless—he concluded—because the soil was too sandy. When Cook got back to the ship he found that "Latouliboula" was sitting in a canoe tied to the ship's stern. " He sat in the Canoe with all that gravity by which he was distinguished at that time, nor could I by any means prevail upon (him) to come into the Ship. The people called him **Arekee** which signifies King, a title I had never hear one of them give Feenough which made me suspect he was not the King."   As noted above, the term 'eiki was applied only to those of very high rank, and was not used for chiefs of the Kanokupolu line, however great their political authority…

The oral history of Tonga does include relatives from other parts of the Pacific. For example, the 'Inasi or presentation of the first fruits to the Tu'i Tonga brought people from Samoa, Fiji and even Tahiti!

It is possible that the so called Tongan Empire of around 1100-1700 included many other Tongan subjects from around the Pacific.

It does support Thor Heyerdahl's theory that the intelligence and skill of the White God's of South America may have given rise to the Tongan (and Samoan) Empire. Tangaloa was also known as the Tu'i Manu'a or King of Manu'a, the most powerful leader in the Samoan group of islands in pre-European times.

Another legend common in Tonga, and shared by some of the other Polynesian islands is the story of Lo'au. He was regarded as a 'foreigner' who was highly intelligent and skilled who instructed the Tongans in many areas including the preparation and drinking of the kava (*Piper methysticum*). Lo'au sailed away from Tonga never to return.

Another similar Tongan legend is of Lepuhaa, who was reputed to have a jellyfish tatooed on the palm of his left hand. Modern interpretations suggest that the jellyfish may have been a compass and Lepuha, like Lo'au was a one of the White Gods, who also sailed away from Tonga and never returned.

Lepuhaa was very popular with women and it is said that when he entered a faikava, he would show the jellyfish on his palm to the tou'a, or woman serving the kava, and she would stand up and follow him, abandoning the kava ceremony. Could the jellyfish be a 'password' between the White Gods? It does seem that the White Gods were responsible for the instruction and construction of the Polynesian including Samoan, Tahitian and Tongan Royal Hierarchy and Culture, and they were living among the people as 'revered beings', but as the legend of Lo'au suggest, they eventually left and never returned. Just like the White Gods of South America.

CHAPTER 5. Tangaloa 'Eitumatupu'a the Tongan legend

The Tongan legend of Tangaroa referred to him as Tangaloa 'Eitumatupu'a in the Tongan language, but this could be referring to 3 people. Tangaloa, 'Aho'eitu and Tupu'a. It is possible that the three of them arrived on a *paepae* from the horizon, perhaps with the white woman Hina or Sina frequently mentioned in other Polynesian legends.

The Tongan legend of Tangaroa starts with Tangaloa 'Eitumatupu'a who was said to be a God who came down from the sky. He had six children.

1. Talafale
2. Tu'i Loloko
3. Maliepo
4. Tu'i Folaha
5. Matakehe

Their mother was a woman named Tamapo'uli

The sixth child was 'Aho'eitu whose mother was Va'epopua 'Ilaheva

She is the daughter of the Tu'i Ha'amea which is the area between Central and Western Tongatapu. This suggest that Tonga was already populated with a social structure when Tangaroa arrived and instigated the Tu'i Tonga Hierachy.

Talafale became the Tu'i Faleua whose grandson is the first Tu'i pelehake and his descendants.

The Tu'i Pelehake

Tu'i Pelehake is one of the most important chiefly titles and estate holders of the Kingdom of Tonga today. The current holder of the title is the grandson of the former King's brother, King Taufa'ahau Tupou IV. He was known simply as Prince Fatafehi Tu'i Pelehake, estate holder of Pelehake Village.

Tu'iloloko, Maliepo, Tu'i Folaha and Matakehe became the Falefa of the Tu'i

Tonga whose task is to provide and protect him.

The Tu'i Loloko gave rise to the first Tu'uhokokilangi and first Malupo of Mu'a, the old capital of the ancient Kingdom.

Maliepo gave rise to the first Lauaki of Talafo'ou.

Lauaki

Lauaki is the King's Undertaker and one of his Chief Spokesperson. He is the estate holder of Talafo'ou Village.

Tu'i Folaha gave rise to the first 'Aholangamakahiva also referred to as 'Aho of Folaha and the first Mailau of Mu'a.

The descendants of Matakehe are believed to be the people who populated the area now known as Folaha, a village in Central Tongatapu.

'Aho'eitu became the first Tu'i Tonga in the year 950, a dynasty of Kings that lasted until 1865 when the last one, Laufilitonga, died.

The Tu'i Tonga had appointed his younger brothers to the titles of Tu'i Ha'a Takalaua and Tu'i Kanokupolu which expanded the Royal Household so much so that there were many disagreements between them.

For example, Taufa'ahau, son of the 17th Tu'i Kanokupolu, Tupouto'a had a disagreement with Laufilitonga, the 39th Tu'i Tonga which resulted in war in 1826-1827. Laufilitonga lost and was stripped of his political power but remained as Tu'i Tonga until his death in 1865, after which the Tu'i Tonga dynasty was abolished.

Taufa'ahau and his victorious Lords formed a new government called the

Kingdom of Tonga in 1875 and he became King George Tupou I. The name George was the name of the British Monarch of the time. There is evidence that Samoans and Fijians had supported Taufa'ahau to beat the Tu'i Tonga. Those Samoan and Fijian Chiefs were appointed by King George in his first government of 1875 to be estate holders in Tonga to this day.

The current ruler of the Kingdom of Tonga is King George Tupou VI.

CHAPTER 6. Another Meaning of the Legend

The modern interpretation of the legend suggest that Tangaloa came from the horizon which also mean sky in ancient Tongan maritime terminology.

The legend claimed he climbed down the toa (ironwood) tree at Popua (eastern tip of Nuku'alofa) where he saw the woman Va'epopua on the beach and he fell in love with her. It is possible that Tangaloa climbed down from a large ocean going vessel on a ladder made of ironwood rather than a tree. Perhaps a paepae, which can be 100 feet long or bigger, with a deck and a cottage on top.

It is known from historical accounts that the Chinese were already building large ocean going vessels, known as 'Dhow', by 950 and were already sailing up and down the coast trading with other countries in the Asian continent. It is possible that these trading vessels came as far as Melanesia and Polynesia as proposed in the DNA evidence.

The alternative is a Chinese invasion. The popularity of the name Tau (Dhow) in Tonga may be a direct result. Tau meaning 'war, arrival, to hang, mooring'…so the people who came from the sky, in the 'Dhow', must have conquered the locals and established the Tu'i Tonga Dynasty.

The prevalence of the Asian mDNA in Tongans, Fijians, Samoans and Maori people, as mentioned before, is evidence that there was 'Asian migrations' to Polynesia, probably through trade.

The name suggest that there were three of them as formerly mentioned. 1. Tangaloa 2. 'Aho'eitu (an expanded form of 'Eitu 3. Tupu'a

It is interesting to note that none of the Tongan Kings or Lords were named after Tangaloa or Tupu'a. However the name 'Aho'eitu has been passed down in Tonga to this day. The current King's birth name was 'Aho'eitu. It is likely that Tangaroa and Tupu'a left but 'Aho'eitu stayed in Tonga.

Tupu'a is a name associated with Samoan Chiefs. The last Samoan Head of State who died in 2017 was Tu'i 'Atua **Tupu'a** Tamasese Efi.

The first **Tupu'a** Tamasese (Titimaea) first appeared in history in 1830 but it is possible the name has been passed down from ancient times.

The name Tangaroa is mostly associated with the Maori people of New Zealand. Tangaroa also appear to have left children in the Cook Islands and Samoa, as well. Tangaroa who became the Tu'i Manu'a in Samoa was probably an offspring. In the Cook islands there was a cult following of Tangaroa and his brothers*.

It is entirely possible that the ocean going boat they were on had gone around the islands and Tupu'a decided to stay in

Samoa, 'Aho'eitu in Tonga and Tangaroa sailed on to other places and New Zealand.

The 'Aho'eitu who became King is probably a nephew of 'Eitu. This is quite common in Tongan genealogy of the ancient Kings. That is, nephews being named after their uncles. Just like the Tangaroa in the Cook Islands and Samoa.

> These are some information from the Victoria University Free New Zealand Text Collection online on Tangaroa

Quote

Tangaroa in the Cook Islands

At the Cook Islands Tangaroa and Rongo are said to have been the twin children of Papa and Vatea, the primal parents. The Rev. Mr Gill tells us that Vatea equals Avatea, and means "noon"; but the Watea of Maori (N.Z.) myth seems rather to personify space. At Mangaia Tangaroa is said to have been really the most important of the twins, but Rongo gained precedence in some way. The Rev. Mr. Gill refers to Tangaroa as the god of day—a peculiar title—and says that his home is in the sky. He believes the cult of Tangaroa, Rongo, and Tane to have been a very old one in the Cook Islands, but that it had been partially obscured by the prominence given to certain deified ancestors. At Mangaia Tangaroa is said to have descended from the heavens by way of the rainbow, and to have here taken to wife one Ina (Hina), and this conjunction we meet with elsewhere. In one old Rarotongan story of Tangaroa the names of Oroio and Roaki are mentioned. These are the Roiho and Roake of Maori myth, two of the offspring of Rangi and Papa, brothers of Tangaroa.

Tangaroa in Tahiti

Ta'aroa (Tangaroa) is viewed at Tahiti as having been the great original god, and with him is associated Hina, of whom we have already spoken. Ta'aroa was the creative being, and the most important, but Tane and Oro (or Koro) were important secondary beings. Cook recognized the importance of Tangaroa at Tahiti, but remarks, "Their prayers are more generally addressed to Tane, whom they suppose to take a greater part in the affairs of mankind."

Tangaloa in Niue

Tangaloa (=Tangaroa) was the principal *atua* of Niue Island, and was there appealed to in connection with war.

Tangaroa in 'Uvea

At Uea, or Uvea (Wallis Island), Tangaloa is said to have dragged up the land from the depths of the ocean, as he did at Tonga, where he is said to reside in the heavens and to be the originator of thunder and lightning. Tregear shows that Tangaloa was also known at Bowditch Island, of the Union Group.

Tangaroa in Samoa

In the Samoan Group Tangaloa is essentially a creator, an original being who formed the islands, or brought them up from the deep. Here also his wife was Hina. Tangaloa dwelt in space, before earth was; he caused land to appear; he caused man to appear, then the heart, then will, then thought. He then caused spirit, heart, will, and thought to enter man, and so man became intelligent. He caused Immensity and Space to bring forth Po and Ao (Night and Day); they produced the sun. He also caused the nine heavens to be formed, and he, Tangaloa, resided in the ninth heaven, where his place of abode was Fale-'ula (Maori, Whare-kura). Turner remarks of Tangaloa at Samoa, "At one place he was seen in the moon, and principally worshipped in the month of May."

Tangaroa in Hawaii

At the Hawaiian Isles Tangaroa bears but an indifferent reputation. He seems to take the place of Miru, Whiro, and Hine-nui-te-po in the subterranean spirit-world. Perhaps he is best compared to Whiro, inasmuch as he represents evil. At the Marquesas Tanaoa (the *r* dropped in this dialect) is said to have represented darkness; from Darkness sprang Atea, and from Atea (Light) sprang Ono (=Rono =Rongo).

Tangaroa in Marquezas

The following passage from Fornander is of interest: "That the Marquesan Tanaoa [Tangaroa] and the Hawaiian Kanaloa [Tanga-roa] embody the same original conception of evil I consider pretty evident. With the Marquesans the idea is treated in the abstract. With them Tanaoa [Marquesan dialect drops *r*] is the primary condition of darkness, chaos, confusion, elevated into a divinity battling with Atea, the god of light and order. With the Hawaiians Kanaloa is the same idea in the concrete, a personified spirit of evil, the origin of death, the prince of Po, the

Hawaiian chaos, and yet a revolted, disobedient spirit, who was conquered and punished by Kane [Tane]."

Unquote

Clearly in the various explanations from the islands of Polynesia of who Tangaroa is, it is nothing more than a legend. A God sometimes with a white woman (Hina or Sina). Was the original Tangaroa, the explorer, accompanied by a fair skinned woman? It is possible that when explorers or conquerors leave on long voyages, they will take their women with them, especially if they are not returning.

References Cited

1. T. Melton, R. Peterson, AJ Redd, N. Saha, AS Sofro, J. Martinson and M. Stoneking. Am J Hum Genet. 1995. Aug; 57(2): 403-414

2. M. Kayser. Silke Brauer, Gunther Weiss, Peter A Underhill, Lutz Roewer, Wulf Schifenhoevel, Mark Stoneking. Current Biology. Vol 10, Issue 20, 14 Oct 2000, p 1237-1246.

2. Journal of the Polynesian Society (online page)

NOTES ON THE AUTHOR

Semisi Pule also known as Semisi Pule Pone, using the short form Semisi Pone (first and last name) was born in the Kingdom of Tonga on 11 December 1961. He attended Longolongo Primary School and Tonga High School where he successfully achieved a 5 subject pass in both the New Zealand School Certificate (1978) and University Entrance Examinations (1979).
He moved to New Zealand in 1980 where he attended the Mt Albert Grammar School and successfully achieved a pass to the University of Auckland. He graduated with a Bachelor of Science in 1985 and returned to Tonga to work for the Ministry of Agriculture, Fisheries and Forests starting June 19, 1985 as an Agriculture Officer/Plant Pathologist.
He returned to New Zealand in 1987 to continue for a Master of Science degree, at the University of Auckland, from which he graduated with Honours in 1989. He, again, returned to Tonga in 1989 to continue his work with MAFF. He was promoted to the position of Senior Plant Virologist in 1991.
In 1992, he joined the University of the South Pacific PRAP 7 project as a Fellow in Tissue Culture. His research with this project is published in the book PLANT PROTECTION IN THE PACIFIC 3, tissue culture and is available from amazon.com

In April 1993, he joined the South Pacific Commission Plant Protection Service as the Co-ordinator and Plant Protection Advisor. He was also appointed to the Biosecurity Committee at the Food and Agriculture Organization of the United Nations for 7 years. In 1994, the South Pacific Conference approved the establishment of the Pacific Plant Protection Organization where he was Acting Chief Executive Officer until the selection and establishment of a new Secretariat.

His work on Plant Protection in the Pacific are published in the series of books PLANT PROTECTION IN THE PACIFIC 1-4 and are available from amazon.com

He migrated with his family to Auckland, New Zealand in June, 1996 where he has been involved in various industries.

He decided to take up writing in 2011 and still carry on with a small business to keep himself exercising and fit.

He has published more than 200 books and ebooks which are all available online from amazon.com, blurb.com and wheelers.co.nz.

www.ingramcontent.com/pod-product-compliance
Lightning Source LLC
Chambersburg PA
CBHW031943070426
42450CB00006BA/871